CHRIST THE VISION

Also by Dom Augustin Guillerand:

Mary the Mirror
They Speak by Silences
Where Silence is Praise

Other Carthusian titles from Gracewing:

Ancient Devotions to the Sacred Heart of Jesus
by Carthusian Monks of the 14–17th Centuries

by a Carthusian:

The Call of Silent Love
Early Carthusian Writings
First Initiation into the Carthusian Life
Interior Prayer
The Prayer of Love and Silence
The Way of Silent Love
The Wound of Love

Carthusian Novice Conferences:

Poor, Therefore Rich
The Freedom of Obedience
From Advent to Pentecost

Saint Bruno The Carthusian
André Ravier SJ

Christ
The Vision

Dom Augustin Guillerand
A Carthusian Monk

Translated from the French
by a Monk of Parkminster

GRACEWING

Originally published in French as *Vivantes Clartés*
by the Benedictines of St Priscilla, Rome, 1964

First published in English in 1966 for the
Carthusian Order in England
by Burns & Oates Ltd

This edition published in England in 2022 by
Gracewing
2 Southern Avenue
Leominster
Herefordshire HR6 0QF
United Kingdom
www.gracewing.co.uk

All rights reserved

Imprimi potest: Fr Ferdinandus
Prior Cartusiæ
In domo Cartusiæ: 8 Decembris 1965

IMPRIMATUR
Antverpiæ, 14 Maii 1966
C.EYKENS,Vic. gen.

© Carthusian Order in England 1966, 2022

ISBN 978 085244 132 9

Cover design by Bernardita Peña Hurtado

TRANSLATOR'S PREFACE

THIS little book[1] presents certain hitherto unpublished writings of the author of *Mary the Mirror*, published in this series in 1963.[2] Like all this contemplative's writings, this present volume consists for the most part of Meditations, written not for publication but because he found it helpful to commit his thoughts to paper while they were fresh in his mind. Even the sermons which follow, although delivered as such to the lay-brothers of the Grande Chartreuse, were really meditations made, so to say, aloud. Those who assisted at them, we are told, never forgot them—not so much for what they said but for what they revealed of, and in, the speaker. In delivering the sermon on the *Paternoster*, he seems to have had the greatest difficulty in getting beyond the first two words: Our Father. As in the case of the great St Teresa, these words alone were sufficient to wrap his spirit in a profound silence, a solitude 'alone with God'; and he lingered over them as though reluctant to let them go.

In one of his writings, this is what he him-

---

[1] *Vivantes Clartés*, published by the Benedictines of St Priscilla, Rome, 1964.
[2] *Mary the Mirror*, by a Carthusian. Published in the Paraclete Series by Burns & Oates, 1963.

self says: "The feasts of the Christian year are hours of union. For most of us, the things that call for mere human activity eat so much into our lives; happy those souls that understand and 'hunger and thirst' to escape their toils. For them, to stop only for a moment, to consecrate some hours at least to look beyond to the deeper movement which carries them on its stream; to fix their heart where there are true joys in the peace of things that do not pass away;[3] to enter into contact with that higher world where one thinks only in order to give oneself, where one finds true repose and joy in a mutual and loving communion, where the unworthiness of all personal interest ceases and no longer claims remembrance or even a name—all this is peace indeed, and rest, a much desired oasis in the desert."

The sermons which comprise the latter part of this booklet are incomplete. No doubt the writer had the intention of taking his hearers through the whole cycle of the liturgical feasts (a subject always dear to him), but his death in April 1945 brought them to a close. Fortunately, either his notes were found or his sermons were remembered and preserved. As sermons they are not perfect. They lack, maybe, that revision which would have given them form; but, imperfect as they are, they reveal something else. Their very repetitions,

[3] Cf. Collect for the Fourth Sunday after Easter: *Ibi nostra fixa sint corda, ubi vera sunt gaudia*... that our hearts may be set where true joy is found.

their steady movement, manifest the slow but penetrating deliberations of the Carthusian at prayer—that 'long regard', as he says elsewhere, 'at the eternal truths'. It is this 'long regard' which is the *motif* which runs through all his writings, all his recorded thoughts. And if we have the courage to follow him in that silent contemplation, we may be fortunate enough to share a little in the light that was given to him, and see something of the depth of the divine truths he was privileged to penetrate.

St Hugh's Charterhouse,
Parkminster,
The Assumption B.V.M., 1965.

CONTENTS

	Page
Translator's Preface	v

MEDITATIONS

Christmas	3
Epiphany	9
Anna the prophetess	15
The Finding of Jesus in the Temple	17
The Hidden Life	24
The Public Life	29
Exaltation of Holy Cross	32

SERMONS

Our Father	37
Who art in heaven	42
Hallowed be Thy Name	49
Candlemas	54
Simeon	58
Ascension	64
Pentecost	69
St John the Baptist	75
All Saints	80

MEDITATIONS

CHRISTMAS

CHRISTMAS is above all a happy and lovely feast. The charm of a cradle envelops it in an atmosphere which attracts and gladdens. Our hearts open out before this Child who is already acquainted with life and its troubles, and is not afraid to encounter them for our sake. His human soul fresh from the hand of God renews ours. The eternal years that preceded his birth have not aged him. He knows all that has been and all that will be, and still he is young like a flower about to open. He preserves the youth of what does not grow old, the youth of an eternal present. From the height of that youth as from an infinite summit, he gives movement to things and communicates his peace to them. Seen by him, they are altogether beautiful and good; seen in him, they appear altogether clothed with that sweetness and beauty.

All the mysteries surrounding the birth of Jesus are suffused with a light from on high, which enhances souls and brings them peace. Always and everywhere we are enabled to see far beyond that which is purely ephemeral and discover depths hitherto unsuspected. A ray which is infinite and eternal emanates from all he says and from all he does. His limitless being is projected into all his actions and in the simplest of his movements. But that light is very varied, and that ray does not colour all it lights up with only one tint. It causes the diversity of scenes to stand out, and awakens in our hearts very different impressions.

Christmas is the festival of joy. *I bring you tidings of great joy*, said the angel to the shepherds.[1] And this joy has travelled down the ages and is always associated with this anniversary. But the joy of Christmas is not just an absence of pain; it does more than make us forget suffering, it makes use of it. The wonderful thing about God is that he knows how to make all things serve his designs. He is infinite joy, and he turns even suffering into joy. That is why the birth of the divine Child is surrounded with trials. Poverty, indifference, contempt, hatred, persecution and exile welcome this newly-born babe. They are not enemies trying to dominate him; they are servants, answering to his call and executing his commands.

Thirty years later, from the mount of the Beatitudes and before immense crowds and with the whole of the human race present to his mind, he uttered aloud his strange secret: *Blessed are the poor in spirit; blessed are the meek; blessed are they that mourn ... that suffer persecution.*[2]

Bethlehem and the humble manger are these

[1] Luke 2. 10.   [2] Matt. 5. 3 ff.

realities, experienced before they were expressed. And that is why we must smile at the infant Jesus, even while he is crying. Not because he weeps, but because he finds joy even in his tears. What is so touching on this earth is not the absence of tears, but the joy born of them. In God there are no contradictions, there is no opposition. To smile and to weep; to be poor or the reverse; to be in trouble or to experience a profound peace—all these things are one in him, since he is greater than them all. He is the infinite summit where all realities unite in the harmony of his love that seeks only what is good, and is sufficiently powerful that when it sees evil it knows how to draw good from it. Christmas is that good thing, that love, that joy restored to our earth and placed at the disposal of all men.

What must we do to enter into possession of these heavenly treasures? We must do what he does who is their master and brings them to us. We must remain detached from them, from his gifts. The reason we do not possess them is that we are possessed by them. Our hearts cannot contain them because they are already filled with a thousand and one things. To be detached does not mean that we have no attachments: it means being attached to something greater than ourselves. Submission to something higher than ourselves is the condition of peace; obedience to what is lower than ourselves is slavery.

We are the sons of God.[3] Our greatness consists in being able to share in his life[4] and to possess our heritage.[5] Anything less than God is too small for us. United with him, we have all; replete with created things, we remain unsatisfied. Subject to him, we are free; attached to creatures, we are slaves. Detachment is thus a liberating, a setting free. The detached soul has broken its bonds and, like a bird, rises up into that atmosphere which is its true element.

This was the burden of the song Jesus heard in his cradle: *Glory to God in the highest, and on earth peace to men of good will.*[6] Too weak to join his voice to that of the angels, he left it to them to make the hill of benediction resound with its message—*glory to God* and *peace to men*. These two phrases and the realities they represent, Jesus came to reunite after long ages of separation. From the time of man's original sin, God and man had been at enmity. Instead of being in concord, they were in opposition. God no longer found in man the glory he looked for from him; man no longer found in God the happiness and peace that only God can give him. Heaven and earth were two kingdoms at war, instead of being a united home.

[3] Cf. Rom. 8. 16. *For the Spirit himself giveth testimony that we are the sons of God.*

[4] Cf. John 10. 10. *I am come that they may have life.*

[5] Rom. 8. 17. *If sons, heirs indeed of God and joint heirs with Christ.*

[6] Luke 2. 14.

Jesus comes... He is at once from heaven and of this earth: he is God, and he is man. He is the link uniting them, the love bringing them together, the life born of these re-established relations. He knows God and he knows man. He knows that God is the creator and master; that all things owe their being to him, and are bound to reflect his glory. He knows that man, the creature, must recognize the divine dominion. He humbles man before God—man: little, poor and obedient, yet at the same time immense, eternal and all-powerful. With one only of his acts, belonging to himself alone, he is able to restore to heaven and earth the exact relationship which will give glory to the Creator and peace to the creature.

In Jesus is united the one to whom adoration is due and those who owe him that adoration. When he adores, all creation bends in adoration to God with him, and yet he is the God whom that creation adores. Thus God receives the glory due to him, and man peace. He is thus seen above all things, more esteemed than all things, more loved than all things. This little child who, in order to give glory to God renounces all satisfaction, thereby manifests his greatness. He renounces all because he knows that he is greater than all; and man is at peace and is supremely content. In returning to God, all his desires are fulfilled; no further desires disturb him, drawing him in different directions. One thought, one desire alone possesses him—God. Detached from all, he possesses all.[7]

And so Christmas stands for that divine detachment which looks beyond the creature and rests in the Creator. And Jesus is the unique being in whom both Creator and creature are united, in order to manifest to the world the realization of that ideal.

---

[7] Cf. 2 Cor. 6. 10. *As having nothing, and possessing all things.*

EPIPHANY

Humble as was his birth, Jesus from the beginning of his life on earth moves the world; he draws souls or repels them. He awakens movements of love and adoration and of mortal hatred. Men come to him from everywhere; all classes are represented at his feet. Simple folk and workers with their hands are among the first, yet the wise ones of the world and those who travail with their spirit are not overlooked. He loves them all, and for all alike his hands and his heart overflow with blessings.

The feast of the Epiphany is the turn of the Wise Men. They come from afar, from the most distant parts. Above all, they come from a totally different environment or state of mind. They are pagans, but their false doctrines awaken no fear in the infant-God, for he is truth dissipating error, and he came precisely to spread truth.

Epiphany is the feast of the light that manifests itself and sheds its rays. It spreads from the hills of Bethlehem, where the angels heralded the light that shone in the dazzled eyes of the shepherds, and still more in their hearts. It traversed plains and valleys, hills and mountains, streams and rivers. It became the Star of the Wise Men, and shone for them in the clear sky of the East. It is the same Star: there is only one light. Whether it is a ray from a star or a light enlightening men's souls, it comes from that Light,[1] and must return to him. And that Light is Jesus, the eternal Word, God of God and Light of light. He gives light to the eyes, and thus to the hearts of men. To the one and to the other he gives himself, and that gift of self is their joy and his joy.

The Gospel does not tell us anything of the emotion experienced by the Wise Men at the sudden appearance of the Star, nor what they felt when they saw the divine Light to whom it led them. For the most part, the Gospel is silent on these more intimate things, probably because mere earthly words would rob them of their beauty, and also so that we may each express them to ourselves in the silence of our hearts. What is certain is that a divine light is constantly arising in our souls, calling us to Jesus. The various scenes depicted in the Gospels are all models, given to us so that we may reproduce them and more or less live them. Our earthly existence is a constant invitation from God to return to him, and in each of the events that go to form that invitation we can recognize a sign from heaven. What we lack is the faith to recognize that sign, and to know how to discover the infinite

---

[1] John 8. 12. *I am the light of the world.*

love under the created forms it takes. God is always speaking to us, but we so seldom recognize his voice.

Why is it that so few saw the Star in the East; why did so few hear the song of the angels? Is it because God revealed his miraculous star only to those few, or reserved his celestial harmonies for the others? Surely not! God offered himself to all men, and desires nothing more than to give himself to all. But he forces himself on no one. Only those eyes that are open, those hearts that are ready to receive him, are able to recognize and welcome him. And only those eyes are opened to the light that know to close them to false lights; just as only those hearts yield to his loving advances that know to turn away from the solicitations of created things. Life's progress is made step by step, by successive stages, and these stages consist of renunciations.

But these renunciations of created things are not made without some sacrifice. What efforts must have been demanded of the Wise Men that they should undertake the long journey which brought them to the feet of the divine King! What those efforts were we do not know, though some of them we can guess. What is certain is that they must have been very great. In those days one did not travel in a *train de luxe*! One needed time; complicated preparations had to be made, and a great burden of organization had to be undertaken.

Moreover, such a journey was not without its dangers. Yet at the mere indication of a mysterious star the Wise Men faced it all. But God surely added to these exterior signs more intimate and reassuring indications, and this double solicitation on his part met with souls of great generosity and faith.

The reward was also a double one, and the Gospel record reveals it to us with great clarity. The first was a negative reward. It consisted in their preservation from all the difficulties of the way. The big obstacle was the want of faith awaiting them in Jerusalem among the Jews whom they consulted. At this distance of time and, accustomed as we are to the story, we no longer perceive this; but in fact the surprise of the Wise Men must have been overwhelming. This birth which had caused them to set out on such a long journey had not even been so much as heard of among the tradesmen of the city, nor was it the subject of conversation in the market-place. Complete indifference, and absolute ignorance of an event destined to raise up souls and transform the world! We can hardly believe that, meeting with such a spirit of indifference in Jerusalem, the Wise Men did not decide to turn back.

The second reward was a positive one. Because of their faith it was given to them to see the Star again. It re-appeared and became their guide; heaven took effective charge of

EPIPHANY

their journey. All they had to do was to follow the light and, thus illumined, the rest of the journey was very short. A few hours of consolation, in which their souls were sustained and, as it were, upheld by grace, and the divine Sun of Justice was there to be seen and contemplated by those who had had the courage to keep faithful to their trust, in spite of all the difficulties, all the delays, all the disappearances of the Star.

And now the divine Sun gives himself, but veiled and, as it were, reduced in splendour. Even at his feet and when he was there before them, only their faith enabled them to recognize and realize that at last they had found him.

This king was revealed as the son of a poor man; this God was but a child. This infinite intelligence is bereft of words, the wonderful love radiating from his heart expresses itself only in cries and inarticulate wailing. The Wise Men are no more troubled by all this than they were by the difficulties and length of their journey, or by the indifference of the Jews. The light shines within them, enabling them to see beyond the swaddling clothes, the silence and the utter poverty. The Star had entered into their hearts, and it allowed them to see with a new light; the divine light shone through all that men despised. Nothing appeared to them greater than this contempt of human contempt, and they adored their sovereign

Master in this little child at the mercy of men and things. Their spirit penetrated the depths of the liberating truth; they knew the All and the nothing, the All commencing where the nothing ceased, when this latter, revealing itself, was dispersed like a mist and gave way before the truth.

For the Wise Men a new day had dawned, in which there was no longer succession of time. All appeared in the light of eternity. And the light of this new day is there before them, giving itself to them under the form of a crying child. Was his hand raised in blessing; did his gaze meet theirs? It matters little. Their faith saw beyond the surface of things, and met and was fused with that infinite love, hidden beneath that surface and rendered more brilliant by it.

ANNA THE PROPHETESS

Her four and eighty years, her long widowhood, her constant fasts and her prayers that persisted in spite of everything,[1] must have given Anna a most glowing and spiritual appearance; the hopes of the Jewish people must have been almost incarnate in her. The walls of the Temple, behind which she had passed her life, had formed her soul as it were in one direction, for one single purpose—the divine service. Beyond that, nothing counted for her. Into such souls, closed to earthly things, heaven pours some strange lights. They are ignorant of much that the world knows, but they know what the world does not know. Like Simeon, Anna is inspired by the Holy Spirit; she is a prophetess. The secrets of heaven are no secrets to her, and the future, when God deems it useful, is open to her eyes like a book.

She comes to the Temple at the very moment that Simeon perceives in the child borne in Mary's arms the Saviour of the world, and in the tender heart of the Mother the sharp sword that will pierce it. And in her own heart, young in spite of her years, a hymn rises as in a Temple. A hymn mounts

[1] Luke 2. 36ff.

to that hidden God revealed to her through her own love. Her joy breaks out in ardent praises; she feels the need to make it known to others. She tells of this Messiah of whose long expected presence she has just become aware. To all those who like her were waiting in expectation of the Redeemer, she announces that the hour has come, and that this tiny child, borne by such humble hands, is indeed the Saviour of the world.

Thus is the divine plan revealed. The silence, the obscurity, the failure on the part of men to recognize him, absorbed as they were in the paltriness of their own affairs, hides him in a kind of veil. But, behind that veil, he who is the light of the world and the all-powerful One, is preparing disconcerting plans that will raise us up again in God. And already, like distant and rapid preludes, light breaks through that veil which hides him, and floods the souls of men of good will, attracted by his infinite tenderness.

THE FINDING OF JESUS IN THE TEMPLE

This incident is a strange one. It presents at least five or six aspects which, humanly speaking, disconcert us. Did Jesus leave his parents when the time came to leave Jerusalem? How did they come to be separated? How was it that his parents set out without him; that they journeyed a whole day without apparently missing him? One could ask any number of such questions, to which one could no doubt give some sort of plausible answer, but which would still leave the mind unsatisfied.

In the life of our Lord, as with nearly all things that happen here below, the final answer to all such questions is that it is the will of God. From eternity, an infinite wisdom has regulated the actions of men and the movements of things, and directs them at every moment in all their details. Without that explanation our minds are constantly up against the unacceptable and even the ridiculous. The Crib and the Cross, and the long years between them, are pure folly to human reason. Only faith, from its point of vantage and from the divine heights from which it views them, finds them infinitely wise and beautiful and good.

Looked at from the point of view of his hidden life, the loss of Jesus in Jerusalem at the time of the Paschal feast appears as an incident from some totally different time. For a few days, our Lord seemed to cease being Mary's son in order to emphasize his divine sonship. This independence in regard to his earthly parents has a double effect. It wounds our hearts, and it shows us once more, among so many other instances, how the realization of the plan of divine love often comes up against the most legitimate of human affections.[1] It reveals the greatness hidden under the most ordinary appearances of this little Galilean boy who resembled all other children of his age, and it also reveals how the precious grace to see beyond these outward appearances is a profound blessing, without which life loses its whole meaning.

Our Lady's grief and that of Joseph are clearly beyond anything we can understand or express. This is the case with all souls at all deep. Silence interprets that grief to a certain extent, at least by telling us that it is beyond words. For our souls are much bigger than our thoughts, and sorrow is a realm which extends far beyond reason. In the case of Mary and Joseph, this realm was almost a vast shoreless ocean.

For they sought to love much more than

[1] Cf. Matt. 10. 37. *He that loveth father or mother more than me is not worthy of me.*

they did to know and to understand. And if they did understand something of the greatness of Jesus, they used that knowledge to feed and increase their love for him. The greatness that their faith perceived in him was, above all, the greatness of his infinite goodness which, under forms so simple and so accessible, gave itself to them and to all men. And that perception deepened in their hearts an ever growing desire to respond to that love. The whole of their being and the whole of their life was concentrated every moment in this single thought and in this single sentiment—he is infinite being communicating himself and longing for us to share in his infinite joy. The fullness, constantly renewed, of these moments in their lives, the unspeakable joy that they experienced in living in such close intimacy with him, is all that one can imagine here below of what life in heaven must be.

And so, one evening, they realized that something of that plenitude was missing; that he who filled their hearts with happiness was not there. Where could he be; why had he left them? A thousand such thoughts troubled them, increasing their sorrow. That sorrow lasted two whole days, for the Gospel tells us: *And it came to pass that after three days they found him in the Temple.*[1] The first day of their return journey, when they thought he

---

[1] Luke 2. 46.

was with them, was Jesus himself without anxiety?[3]

Thus the Son who is love itself, whose heart was infinitely tender and delicate, asked of their hearts into which he had poured that delicate tenderness, at a time when they least expected it and under conditions particularly distressing, the heavy trial of losing him. From all eternity, knowing their love and foreseeing their deep sorrow, he deliberately prepared and planned, he himself alone, that cross that was to be laid upon their shoulders. It was almost more than they could bear. Our Lady did not attempt to hide it under a heroic attitude manifestly false. She had suffered terribly, and she said: *Why hast thou done so to us? Behold, thy father and I have sought thee sorrowing.*[4]

Our Lord did not reproach them for their sorrow. He willed the sweet expression they gave to it; he welcomed it from a heart that was deeply moved. He was pleased with a sad joy to hear on the lips of his Mother these words that went straight to his heart. But he had foreseen that sorrow in the hierarchy of sentiments to which his life and his role as Saviour was to bear witness. And in that hierarchy he had placed this love for his earthly parents second. The first, higher even than the happiness of his Mother's heart, was his Father's glory. Stronger than the happi-

[3] Luke 2. 44. [4] Luke 2. 48.

ness of rejoicing the heart of his Mother, he willed the restoration of the honour due to God. *How is it that you sought me*, he said to her; *did you not know that I must be about my Father's business?*[5]

Hitherto, his Father's business and the submission due to his parents had not clashed. And for long years still that harmony would take its happy course and continue. But if it did not press, it could not last. And Jesus had willed that suddenly his loved ones should be aware of it, even if it meant breaking their hearts. The higher authority of his heavenly Father had spoken, and the Son had obeyed. And Mary and Joseph, submissive and trusting, had known the frightful martyrdom of the separation which was to presage so many others.

The occupation of Jesus in the Temple during these three days is no less strange than the mystery of his remaining far from his loved ones. He was *in the midst of the Doctors*.[6] He listened to them and questioned them. His attitude was what one would expect of one of his age. He did not pose as a master, he remained a child. But even so, his divinity shone through. He astonished, indeed he stupefied them. Those who heard him were amazed at his replies to the questions they put to him.[7] And so he appears always in that dual character, of which one resembles ours,

[5] Luke 2. 49.   [6] Luke 2. 46.   [7] Luke 2. 47.

whilst the other reveals his divinity. For that, indeed, was what he was—man and God, the God-man.

And from this derives the effect his actions have on men. He convinces without frightening, he commands belief without repelling. He draws and wins souls as much as he claims submission. He appears as one of us and, at the same time, he is apart from us, superior to us. He acts thus as a mediator.[*] His human nature places him on our level, while his divinity raises us up to that state we have lost and must get back. Children see him as a child like themselves, listening and asking questions just as they do. Learned people like the doctors in the Temple discover in him depths of understanding compared with which their knowledge is like a drop of water. A drop of water and a vast ocean—Jesus is both.

According to men's circumstances and needs, Jesus appears under these divers forms. A tiny white host lost, so to speak, in the silence of the Tabernacle, which sacrilege can profane; outraged by the impious, despised by the indifferent, forgotten by the world—he remains there alone, for long hours, without a glance or a thought to console him. He would appear to be the most impoverished and forsaken upon earth. And yet, where is the prince, the *savant*, the warrior or the artist of his time who has left a trace comparable to

[*] Cf. 1 Tim. 2. 5.

his history? For whom have men laid down their lives, and do so still? To whom do they pray in times of distress? Whose name do mothers repeat to their children in the cradle; what name consoles the dying as they lie on their bed of suffering?

THE HIDDEN LIFE

ONE sentence sums up in its simple yet striking expression the adolescent years of Jesus—*he was subject to them.*[1] He placed himself under his parents, conducting himself in their regard as one obedient in all things.

In what did that submission consist; how was it reflected in his actions? The Holy Spirit is silent on this point. He has treated these divine manifestations of his subjection (which occupied the greater part of his earthly existence) as though they were of no interest. Our personal imaginations can conjure up all sorts of ideas on the subject, and they have not failed to do so. We think of him as cutting wood and planing it, and fashioning the pieces into farm instruments. We see him under the tender glances of Mary and Joseph in the evenings after the day's work was done, silent, loving, living an interior life which his active life fed but did not disturb. It is interesting to watch the movement of that dual life, given to God yet given to men, to things, to all creation —and to its author, uniting all in a disposition so simple that it was not apparent because nothing could express it.

But this effort to understand Jesus is good,

[1] Luke 2. 51.

and our surmises are salutary. The Gospel, however, tells us nothing on the matter. It is sufficient, it says, to know that Jesus obeyed his parents; for it is not a question of what one does but of the spirit in which one acts.

What was his spirit? He put into all he did his whole spirit, his whole soul, the soul of a God-man. It was the spirit of one who thought, felt and spoke as we do, but who did all in God. These words do not tell us much—how does God think, love and act? In order to know this, we must see him at work, and the whole of that part of his life is hidden.

Nevertheless the answer is there—in that obscurity, in that silence. God is a hidden God.[1] He is shy of drawing men's attention to himself. He wants the attention but he does not like the way men usually go about it. He reveals himself, speaks and draws men's attention openly, but only for relatively short periods. In all it amounted to a tenth of his life on earth—three out of three and thirty years. And even during those three years, he hid himself and spoke less rather than more. He was at no pains to spread the knowledge of his words or of his actions. He found a way of making his public life a new manifestation of his love for the hidden life.

For that matter, true life is always hidden. Public life, as in our Lord's case, is only the hidden life slowly manifesting itself. If it is not

[1] Cf. Isa. 45. 15. *Verily, thou art a hidden God.*

that, it is not true; it allows itself to be taken for what it is not. It is agitation—on the surface. True life is essentially a deep, interior movement. Whether it manifests itself exteriorly or remains hidden, it is life. It is life because it is true action, and not merely agitation. Throughout the long, silent and obscure years of his submission to his parents, Jesus was the unperceived but the real Redeemer of men.

His hidden life had a sequel. Again the Gospel sums it up in two words—*he grew*.[a] It was his act of submission that made him grow. It was, in fact, the effect of life, of life developing. If at any moment of our life our growth ceases, it is because the forces of mortality are greater than those of life. Jesus did not know this second period, that of a decrease of strength. For him, death was not to come from within but from without, and then only when he gave the word. He grew, then, because he was *subject*, and that subjection was the result of order.

Now order is the essential condition of life, which in turn is the harmonization of the forces of being, uniting and concurring to assure development. Life is an opening out resulting from that harmony, just as death is the result of intestine strife between these same forces, but disunited and at war with one another.

Death is the result of revolt; life is born of

[a] Cf. Luke 2. 52. *And Jesus advanced in wisdom and age.*

submission to order. The divine obedience of Jesus at Nazareth brought man back to his lost order, and life flowed in him as a result. Our Lord's public life made this clear. It was to express in words what the hidden life was intended to make implicit in acts. And the words could only be understood in the light of the acts that preceded them.

Words are terms; they explain acts, just as acts manifest the hidden life. At first nascent and passive in his Mother's womb, Jesus began to act in the workshop at Nazareth, and finally spoke in the fields of Galilee and on the steps of the Temple at Jerusalem. His Passion was his crowning act, for it was an act again silent and impersonal, where being seemed to turn back on itself in order to concentrate on the deeper life. And the Eucharist is the prolongation of that movement, bringing together into a state of absolute helplessness all that has preceded it.

The same life runs through them all. In all, Jesus is the Son turned towards his Father and living by this relationship. It is this, his life-giving submission, which makes him grow constantly, and will one day lead him (when all the elect are reunited with him in this filial relationship) unto that *perfect man, unto the measure of the age of the fullness of Christ.*[4]

For the hidden life of Christ will last until the end of time, and will always be his true

[4] Ephes. 4. 13.

life. For each of us also, it will not be the words or the external manifestations which will have the greatest effect on our growth, but the interior disposition from which they proceed, and which animates them.

Ah the mystery of that long life hidden in souls, echo of the hidden life of the Tabernacle and its *raison d'être*! How it is the object of all God does in our regard! One cannot think of it, meditate on it and endeavour sufficiently to penetrate it. Jesus of Nazareth, the young boy subject to and obedient to his parents, saw it in the silent obscurity of his first thirty years, and he knew that he would be an even a greater mystery as the Saviour sadly misunderstood, whom the greater part of mankind would pass by—not with hatred or wickedness, but simply unconcerned; seeing in him only an ordinary workman, too conscientious to make a success of his life!

THE PUBLIC LIFE

JESUS is now thirty years of age. Thirty years of silence and of the hidden life, of recollection and union with his Father, of submission and work; years opposed to the spirit of the world which is pride, agitation and pleasure. Thirty years, that is, most instructive and redemptive.

Had his mission ended there, he would have been content, he could not have wished for more. For there had been no self-will, no designs of his own. He had willed what his Father willed;[1] he had desired only what his Father desired. He had set out to accomplish to the least detail his Father's plans,[2] and in so doing he had found complete peace and joy in that union of desire, that harmony of will, that perfect oneness of heart. Now his Father wills that our salvation should be accomplished by a period of public life, of preaching, of miracles—in a word, by an exterior activity which was to draw men's attention to himself.

For him, it was an immense sacrifice. We know so little of our Lord's soul that we do not notice this. The surroundings in which he

---

[1] Cf. John 14. 31. *As the Father hath given me commandment, so do I.*
[2] John 17. 4. *I have finished the work which thou gavest me to do.*

had lived up to now were humble, no doubt, but they were wonderfully peaceful and dear to the Master who said of himself that he was *meek and humble of heart*.[3] Mary and Joseph, their souls deep and simple, formed for him, as it were, a heavenly defence, wherein he breathed the atmosphere of his true homeland.

And now Joseph was to disappear from the scene as quietly as he had lived. The tender affection of the divine Son and of the beloved Mother had together drawn closer the ties that bound him to them (were that possible), and had rendered dearer and more intimate a relationship that had become more necessary. And it is just then that his Father's plan demanded separation.

Now we are inclined to represent our Lord as a being altogether supernatural. This is quite false. He was perfect God, but he was also perfect man. He had a heart like ours, and a sensitivity like ours. The only difference was that, in his case, the heart and the sensitivity were completely intact and *set in order*.[4]

And because they were intact they were extremely delicate; and because they were 'ordered' they were subject to powers higher than themselves, namely reason and God. He experienced, therefore, all our joys and all our sorrows. He experienced them just as we do but with a delicateness of one whose sensitivity

---

[3] Matt. 11. 29.
[4] Cf. Cant. 2. 4. *He hath set in order charity in me.*

had not been blunted, and who responded immediately and without loss to the impressions made on him.

We have tried to record the feelings of Jesus and of Mary at this hour of separation. We must remember that those feelings would have been very similar to those we experience in similar circumstances, but in a measure and with a particular intensity that no effort of ours of word or imagination can reproduce.

And so his public life began—a new life, with nowhere to shelter,[5] and no one to whom he could unburden himself and who would understand. And yet a life more loved because it was more completely sacrificed to one end, the glory of the Father.

---

[5] Cf. Matt. 8. 20. *The Son of man hath not where to lay his head.*

EXALTATION OF HOLY CROSS

THE Cross is raised up by Jesus. He threw upon it a light which revealed it as something great, something immense, covering the whole world, and lighting it up with a light that transformed it. Before this the world had become quite tiny, it could no longer raise itself up. And men and things remained within themselves, confined in their narrowness. Things no longer gave themselves up to men; men had to take them by sheer force; they failed to submit. There was war throughout the whole of creation: such was the law. The mighty current of love which circulated in the divine work had been brought to a standstill by sin. Things would have liked to give themselves to God through man, but instead they gave themselves to man for man. Man was not their end because he was not their beginning. By keeping them, therefore, for himself, by keeping himself for himself, man had become a usurper and a tyrant. Things were in revolt among themselves, and man was in revolt with himself. This was only to be expected. Shut up within itself, the created world had become narrow and mean; it had been dethroned; it had lost all the divine expansion which had made it immense and, in a way, infinite.

The Cross restored that contact. And by the Cross I do not mean the wood nor its form, not even the suffering it represented, but the movement which was effected in its arms. Christ had taken the Cross on his shoulders; the Cross had taken Christ in its arms. From that marriage came a new light, a new love, a new order, a new life, a new greatness for the Cross, for the world, even for God.

The raising up of the Cross was the raising up of everything. The whole world was again set upright,[1] and re-established in its former greatness. A breath from the spirit of God passed anew over it,[2] and it became one again in the light which was the Light raised up and which, coming from God, returned to God.

The Cross is luminous. It was not the light, but it bore in its arms him who is the *Light of the world*.[3] It gave him to those who looked at it, and that light was born in them and they became *children of light*.[4] It was the light that gave birth to them, for it was *the light of life*.[5] It gave itself to those who turned towards it, and who in turning to it turned away from darkness. Their souls became mirrors, and the light reproduced itself therein. They gave themselves not merely that they might behold that light, but that they might welcome it; that they might become transformed into that

---

[1] Cf. Eccles. 7. 30. *God made man upright.*
[2] Cf. Gen. 1. 2. *And the spirit of God moved over the waters.*
[3] Cf. John 8. 12. *I am the light of the world.*
[4] John 12. 36. [5] John 8. 12.

light. It is within themselves that they behold it, nevertheless it is the light they see for they have become what it is and they do what it does . . . because it is light of life.

The light of life is a light which manifests itself in giving itself, and gives itself in manifesting itself. Its action is perceived in this gift of self, in the movement that follows in those who receive it. It is this movement which makes it known, for it is a movement that takes place in a living person; it comes from him and yet remains within him. It is a movement characteristic of a life which is light, for it is the movement of Light himself. One sees therefore in this single movement both one and the other: the life by the light, the life in the light, and the light in the life. *In him was life, and the life was the light of men.*[6]

[6] John 1. 4.

SERMONS

OUR FATHER

THE Lord's Prayer—the *Our Father*[1]—is the perfect prayer, the prayer of prayers, and sums up all others. It establishes between the soul and God a relationship which is strictly and truly eternal life.

When we sincerely utter the word *Father*, and put into it all the meaning of which it is capable; when, in uttering it, we keep turned well away from all that is not God and completely turned towards him alone; when, by the light of faith, we see clearly the movement of this Father, pouring into our souls his life and being, reproducing in us his features and making us his children in his image and likeness;[2] when, to our great delight, we see these features growing in us; when, in a word, we give ourselves as he gives himself—then we may be quite sure that the three Persons of the Blessed Trinity are there within us, knowing one another, loving one another and giving themselves to one another as they do in heaven. Consequently, that heavenly life, which we call eternal or divine life, increases within us, and the infinite happiness which is that life enters into our soul—it is true, under a veil,

[1] Matt. 6. 9ff.
[2] Gen. 1. 26.

the veil of faith,[2] but none the less really. We should think well on this.

That is why a soul, when drawn by grace, finds its complete happiness in the *Paternoster*, and even, though obviously rarely and by exception, in no more than the first word which says all. In giving us this prayer, however, the divine Master added other words, not in order to change anything or to complete it, but to present it in a more vivid light.

Notice we do not say just *Father*, or *my* Father, but *our* Father. The word *our* has a double meaning. It signifies first of all possession—that one has the free disposal of something; it is a possessive pronoun. In this setting, it signifies that the Father to whom we are speaking is truly our Father; he belongs to us, and we treat him accordingly. (This is an amazing truth, but it is true.) The Church is aware of this astonishment when, in the Mass, just before the *Paternoster*, it places on the lips of the celebrant the words: *Emboldened by the saving precepts of the Redeemer, and following his divine command, we dare to say: Our Father . . .* This courage, this boldness, we not only may, but must possess. God is truly our Father, and he wants us to give him this title. He himself has given us the right to employ it, and to pronounce this name. This right is not ours by nature. By nature, we are his creatures, his servants. The

[2] Cf. 1 Cor. 13. 12. *Now I know in part.*

title of 'son' or 'child' is God's free gift, a grace absolutely unmerited. Never, had he not taught it us, would we have known to employ it. But he used it and he willed it. He wills that we act in his regard as children; that our relations with him are those of a son towards a father; that we make his heart our resting place.

The pronoun *our* has another meaning, connected very intimately with the first. We are not his only son—there was only one, his perfect Image, in whom he was completely reproduced.[4] We become *sons of God*[5] if we dwell in him. Hence those invitations of Jesus: *Come to me*[6] ... *abide in me.*[7] Hence also his prayer: *Father, that they may be one, as we also are one: I in them, and thou in me.*[8] If we respond to these appeals, then he lives in us and we in him; we make but one. *And I live, now not I, but Christ liveth in me.*[9]

Immediately we can see what follows from this. Our voice is no longer merely 'ours', it is the voice of the Beloved that delights the Father: in hearing it, he hears his Beloved Son.

There is yet another consequence, or rather that consequence can be seen under a larger and more permanent aspect. The sacred Scriptures call Christ the *first-born amongst many brethren.*[10] He has himself told us who

---

[4] Cf. Matt. 17. 5. *This is my beloved Son.*
[5] Cf. John 1. 12. *He gave them power to be made the sons of God.*   [6] Matt. 11. 28.   [7] John 15. 4.   [8] John 17. 22-23.
[9] Gal. 2. 20.   [10] Rom. 8. 29.

these brethren are, in a circumstance and in words we can never tire of recalling. *Who is my mother, and who are my brethren? . . . Whosoever shall do the will of my Father.*[11] The 'doing of the will', the keeping of the word, is what gives us this family likeness. For the Word is the Son, the likeness of the Father. Those who keep his word and love it, give birth to him within them; they reproduce that likeness in which they were made, and so make one with Jesus. When, therefore, we sincerely say these words *Our Father*, we are not alone; an immense concourse is with us, in Jesus and with Jesus. *I in them, and thou in me. He gave them power to be made the sons of God.*

That is why the word *our* is necessary. It expresses an idea which gives to our prayer and to our soul an immense grandeur. All heaven and all earth, all the celestial family, the Holy Trinity, the angels and the saints pronounce it with us. Such is the meaning of our Lord's words: *That they may be one, as we also are one.*

You see, or rather you perceive (for what I am saying is only a very tiny part of the reality) how great we are when we say this word *Paternoster*, and how we must say it with our whole mind, our whole heart, our whole strength and with complete joy, because it is the song of life.

[11] Matt. 12. 48, 50.

It is most important to remember that all this is real, as real as the things we see with our eyes, indeed even more so. It is this conviction that souls lack. It is this conviction that has made the saints and kept them so long at their prayers. It is this that was the secret of our Lord himself and of the Holy Family; and it is this that will constitute heaven for us. This conviction, its deep and living character, depends both on God and on us. To acquire it we need grace, and it grows with repeated practice.

God gives this grace if we are ready to receive it. The putting into practice of this conviction disposes the soul to receive it still more. A soul that often renews its act of faith in the divine fatherhood, in the divine presence, that constantly thinks of him, is a soul to whom God gives himself, and that soul is able to say with Jesus: *He hath not left me alone, for I do always the things that please him.*[12]

[12] John 8. 29.

WHO ART IN HEAVEN

LET us continue meditating together on that lovely prayer the *Our Father*, which sprang from the very heart of Jesus and is its perfect expression. The divine lips were the first to utter it, but many are the souls since then throughout the ages that have repeated it, and meditated on it after him. How often have we not ourselves repeated it and meditated on it, and how often will not others after us do the same, and so on to the end of time. And yet no one has ever plumbed its depthless beauty, or ever will do so.

At once the *Paternoster* places us in the presence of God. No more hesitations, no more side-tracking, no more complications: immediately we are 'in contact'. And only the eternal Son could know and reveal this contact to us. For it is his own secret—the relationship which exists between the Father and the Son. We call him *our Father*: the Father who gives us life, who safeguards that life in us; who sustains us, feeds us, inspires and protects us unceasingly with vigilance and care and with all the tenderness that we could wish for.

This relationship allows us to enter into his inner sanctuary; it makes us, as it were, one of the family. It unites us with the divine Son and through him with all those who are moved by the same spirit. It unites us with Mary, the Mother of the divine Son and our Mother, with the angels and the saints, with all the celestial choir, all the inhabitants of that heavenly City where there is no division, no hatred, no jealousy, no self-love, but only an all-embracing love which makes its citizens of one mind and of one heart. That is why we say, not merely *Father*, but *Our Father*.

That 'home', that place where we shall find our 'family' waiting to welcome us, is heaven, the dwelling-place and the house of God. We do not have to seek it far away. Our Lord himself said so explicitly: When you pray, there is no need to leave your house and go out into the public streets.[1] On the contrary, enter into the most retired, the most secret, the most silent and intimate room of your own home. In other words, *enter into thy chamber, and pray to thy Father in secret*.[2] If he hides himself, it is only because he is waiting for you there. He invites you there, he draws you in order to welcome you, to listen to you, to enjoy the role of a father who wants to spread among his children the light that is his life. That is what heaven is—the soul's secret inner sanctuary, the great depths, the centre, the soul's most

[1] Cf. Matt. 6. 5. *When ye pray ye shall not be as the hypocrites that love to stand and pray in the synagogues and corners of the streets that they may be seen by men.*
[2] Matt. 6. 6.

hidden retreat, far from the outside, from all movement, from all noise. God is there, and from that inner sanctuary he gives himself, he radiates his enlightening and vivifying love. It is there we shall find him, there he calls us, there the dwelling-place of the Father. It is there the divine Master leads us in order that he may speak to us and unite us with him. This was the whole of his teaching, the one theme to which he returned again and again so as to impress it always more deeply; and it was around this theme that his discourse after the Last Supper turned. *If any man love me,* he said, *he will keep my word; and my Father will love him, and we will come to him and make our abode with him.*[1]

And our Lord introduces us into this dwelling-place when we pronounce the words *Our Father, who art in heaven.* We must come there often, and stay there as long as we can in the greatest intimacy: alone, silent, indifferent to everything else, to all that is so transitory and ephemeral; alone with him, in his presence, held by his love, filled with the life he is unceasingly giving us, and as unceasingly repeating the word which says all—*Father!*

Why do we not stay longer in this inner sanctuary of the soul, his dwelling-place? Why do we leave it without any reason, or for reasons that are so futile? What can we do to stay there longer? These are questions a

[1] John 14. 23.

religious must often ask himself, and which he is obliged to answer sincerely if he also, in spite of the conditions of his life which are so favourable, and in spite of his vows, is not to waste a time that is so precious, a time intended to strengthen his filial ties with God. If he does not face this question he will expose himself to say with those who have wasted their lives, that bitter word of disillusion which the sacred Scriptures place on the lips of the unjust: *We have erred from the way of truth.*[4]

These first words of the *Paternoster*, as I have said, can suffice. A soul drawn to them can rest in them, repeating them again and again, and so make an excellent prayer. For these words contain implicitly all that follows, all that one can say to God. Nevertheless, our Lord thought it as well to complete them by indicating what we should ask our heavenly Father for, and in what order.

Our Lord's prayer contains seven requests, divided into two groups. The first three requests are for God's sake, the remaining four for ours. As regards the former, it is just—indeed, it is necessary—that God should be the very first consideration. We must think of him first, and then only of ourselves.

For him, we ask three things—the glory of his name, the advancement of his kingdom, and the accomplishment of his will. *Hallowed be thy name; thy kingdom come; thy will be done*

[4] Wis. 5. 6.

on earth as it is in heaven.[5] We ask first for the glory of his name, that it be hallowed, that is, glorified. Now God has two names, and he gave them to him himself. One is in the Old Testament, before the coming of his divine Son, the Redeemer, the other after, in the New Testament. In the Old Testament, he revealed his being, in the New his love.

Under the ancient Law, God said to Moses: *I am who am.*[6] The circumstances in which these words were spoken are well known. Moses was in the desert, guarding his sheep. His was a soul deeply pious. The account in the Scriptures does not tell us this, but it is clear that his spirit was 'with God'. Suddenly, he noticed a burning bush. He watched it attentively: the bush was burning without being consumed. He approached it. A voice spoke from the flames: *Come not nigh hither. Put off thy shoes from thy feet, for the place whereon thou standest is holy ground.*[7] And then the voice confided to him his mission to save his people, and it told him how he was to go about it. In the event, Moses, frightened at the idea of a mission which he realized was beyond his powers, asked who it was that spoke to him. And that was the answer: *I am who am. Say to those who question you: HE WHO IS hath sent me to you.*[8]

With the Incarnation, when the Son of God

[5] Matt. 6. 9-10. [6] Exod. 3. 14. [7] Exod. 3.5.
[8] Exod. 3. 14.

became like unto us, clothed with our nature, the whole tone and attitude changed completely. *God is love,* says St John.[9] In him there is only love. He so loved the world that he sent his only begotten Son to save it.[10] He is also a father, and when we speak to him we say: *Our Father.*

Under these two names God must be 'sanctified', that is to say, glorified. The word 'saint' means 'separated'. To sanctify means to separate, to distinguish, to place apart. To sanctify God's name, therefore, means to separate it, to distinguish it from every other name. God wills this; he cannot do otherwise. The Scriptures emphasize this again and again: I am not like the rest of creation...I am 'other'. *My thoughts are not your thoughts, nor your ways my ways.*[11] I am the Master: *I am who am.*

Note well this expression, which is so unusual. Or rather, it would be unusual, if it did not refer to God, who is *being*: but it is wonderful since it does so. *I am who am*: that is to say, in me there is only *being.* In everything and in everyone else there is a mixture of being and 'nothingness'. We are here today, but we were not here a hundred years ago, and we shall not be here a hundred years hence. We are here, in this particular place, but not elsewhere; we can only be in one place at a time. Similarly, we are subject to change; we are not what we

[9] 1 John 4. 16.   [10] Cf. John 3. 16.   [11] Isa. 55. 8.

shall be in so many years time. Our body is weak, our mind is limited; our reason can take strange turns, and our will is not stable. We are *this* person, *this* religious; to make ourselves understood we have to make use of any number of limitations, and these limitations are, as the word indicates, limits that determine the tiny part of being, of time, place, intelligence, will and life, of any 'good' that we possess. In God there is nothing of this. In him, there is no limit of time, place, life, intelligence, power or of any 'good'; he is boundless, without limits. We cannot imagine what this means, since we have no terms of comparison. We can only say what he is not.

HALLOWED BE THY NAME

WHEN we have truly entered into God's presence; when we have given him the name which indicates our true relationship with him; when, having pronounced that name which opens his heart to us whom he loves as his children, and our heart has responded with a movement of filial love; when we have rejoined this Father in the great depths of our soul, in that inner sanctuary, secret, silent and remote, which is his dwelling-place within us; when, by an effort of recollection, we have concentrated all our thoughts on him and have forced ourselves to see only him who looks at us and gives himself to us; when we have reunited all these dispositions in the first words of the Lord's Prayer, *Our Father, who art in heaven*—then we can begin our prayer of requests.

We say: *Hallowed be thy name*. Note again this word 'hallowed' or sanctified. To sanctify is, as we have said, to separate. A saint is one who separates himself from creatures, from all that is worldly and transitory, in order to dedicate himself to the things of God and to the realities that do not pass away. The earth and all that pertains to it no longer count. The saint places himself above them; he dominates them, he raises himself up. Instead of being at their mercy, dependent upon them, he frees himself—he is free of them; he is their master, greater than them all.

Now it is precisely this that is God, only in a measure and perfection incomparable. That is his greatness. In Holy Scripture he tells us this, and repeats it himself in almost every line: *I am the Lord.*[1] Creatures are no more than tiny drops of dew compared to the shoreless ocean of his being. According to the Psalmist, they are even less than that; they are as nothing. And he adds elsewhere: *A thousand years in thy sight are as yesterday, which is past.*[2] What remains of the day once it is past? A memory, and a memory which is already passing and is quickly and completely lost in the dust of the years and of subsequent events, like a landscape that has faded. This is what the whole world is in God's sight.[3]

Therein is his glory. He has a right to it, and claims that right. He does not want to be confounded with his work. He wills to remain apart, that his name be separated, distinguished from all else. He wills that when we pronounce that name we see it as that of our Lord and Master,[4] one superior to all and everything. Holy Scripture is full of this thought. In the Divine Office, above all in the Psalms, we meet

---

[1] Cf. Gen. 28 and Exod. 32 *passim*.
[2] Ps. 89. 4.
[3] Cf. Ps. 143. 3. *Lord, what is man, that thou art (mindful of) him.* [4] Cf. Matt. 23. 10. *For one is your Master, Christ.*

with it constantly under different forms. And if we give this thought the attention it deserves, the thought is always the same.

Now, as he have already said, God made himself known to men under two names—*I am who am*, and *God is love*. But he has not only said it, but he revealed it in his acts and works. God has accomplished two great acts, and he has done two principal works. The two acts are creation and the Incarnation, the two works nature and grace. Creation communicated his being and made us and all creation his creatures; grace communicated his life and made us—and us alone among all his works—his children. Nature reveals God's first name: *I am who am*; grace makes known his second: 'I am love; I am a Father'.

God's first name is *He who is*. He *is*, from all eternity to all eternity. He did not receive being from anyone; he had it in himself, of himself and by himself, and it is his pristine glory, the essential trait which distinguishes him from us, his creatures.

If, when you look at a rose or at any object in general and I ask you what it is called, you reply: 'It is', I would at once ask you again: But what *is* it? Merely to say that *it is* is not enough, it tells me nothing. To define it you must tell me what kind of being it is. Anything created is always this or that particular thing.

But God is not a particular being. His being is just what it says—*being*: that is his definition.

To define a thing is to set limits to it. But God has no limits, he is all there is of being. He is all that is and can be, all that is actual and all that is possible. Yet he is not the sum total of all beings, but their source. The source is constantly pouring itself out, but it remains always the source.

In the same way God is the source of all that exists; the world is, as it were, his being extended outside of himself, a kind of overflow. The world is his work—the heavens and the earth, the light and the great stars that reflect it, the earth and all that it consists of—mountains, plains, the great oceans, all living things, plants and flowers, trees with their innumerable scents, the birds of the air and the fishes of the sea, the animals that people the globe. All this array so varied is ceaselessly and untiringly studied by man in order that he may master it and make it serve his designs; and yet he knows so little about it! Such is God's handiwork.[5] He could have done much more, he could also have done nothing at all. His being would have remained the same, neither diminished nor increased.

And that work is marvellous. It is marvellous as a whole, in the order which prevails in it; in the movement of the numberless planets, much greater than our earth, which circulate in space at an incredible speed, yet without clashing in the services they render one an-

[5] Cf. Ps. 18. 2.

other. Scientists ask themselves whether the detailed study of a single star, even the smallest, is not more wonderful still. When they study the constitution of a rock crystal or that of a plant, a flower, a wild anenome or a hedgerow violet—all reveal a power, a wisdom, a capacity of mind able to conceive such things, and a precision in the execution which is utterly beyond them and is overwhelming...

And God has made not only a single blade of grass, but all the flowers, and all the stars that fill the universe. He is their unique source, their creator, and he conserves them in being. He made them, and he watches over them ... I could continue long on this theme without ever exhausting it ... We sing of this constantly in the Divine Office, especially at night at Lauds. It is the whole burden of our song: *All ye works of the Lord, praise and exalt him above all for ever ... Let the earth bless the Lord, let it praise and exalt him above all for ever.*[6]

[6] Cf. Dan. 3. 57ff.

CANDLEMAS

UNDER the symbolic title of Candlemas, the feast we are keeping today is very specially the feast of light. In reality all the mysteries of the holy Childhood and all the feasts which recall it are literally bathed in that light. On Christmas Day we echo like a refrain the prophecy of Isaias concerning the people of Galilee: *The people that walked in darkness have seen a great light; to them that dwell in the region of the shadow of death, light is risen.*[1] On the feast of the Epiphany, the same voice repeats the same news to Jerusalem and Judæa: *Arise and be enlightened, O Jerusalem, for thy light is come, and the glory of the Lord is risen upon thee.*[2] Light awoke the shepherds on the hillsides of Bethlehem, and it shone in the sky in the East for the Wise Men. It was the same light that Simeon in his old age saw and hymned with a full heart in the Temple at Jerusalem. *Now thou dost dismiss thy servant, O Lord, in peace, because my eyes have seen the light that will be for the salvation of the Gentiles, and the glory of thy people, Israel.*[3]

What exactly is this light, and what do we see by it? It has illumined life, says St Paul in effect.[4] And St John, even more precisely: *In*

---
[1] Isa. 9. 2. [2] Isa. 60. 1. [3] Luke 2. 29-32.
[4] Cf. 2 Tim. 1. 10. *But is now made manifest by the illumination of our Saviour, Jesus Christ.*

CANDLEMAS 55

the beginning was the Word, and in him was life, and that life was the light of men.[5] It could hardly have been put more clearly. That *true light which enlighteneth all men,*[6] which the prophets had foretold and the shepherds, the Wise Men, Simeon and Anna, all had seen—that light was the life of the *Word made flesh,*[7] of the Son of God, the life of *the only begotten Son who is in the bosom of the Father.*[8]

This life, the Word, the light that appeared amongst us in order that we might know it and share in it, has been described for us in terms that could not be simpler or more to our hand. *The Son,* says St John, *cannot do anything of himself, but what he seeth the Father doing; for what things soever he doth, these the Son also doth in like manner.*[9] He is the perfect image, the *brightness of his glory and the figure of his substance;*[10] *the unspotted mirror of God's majesty, and the image of his goodness.*[11] *For the Father loveth the Son,* continues St John, *and sheweth him all things which himself doth.*[12] This, and this alone, is what the Son, the perfect mirror of the Father, does. The Father loves and is constantly manifesting that love, and the Son does likewise. And that love is life.

Here, of course, we touch upon the interior life of the Blessed Trinity, and no words of ours can ever express that mystery. In that

[5] John 1. 1ff. [6] John 1. 9. [7] John 1. 14
[8] John 1. 18. [9] John 5. 19. [10] Heb. 1. 3. [11] Wis. 7.26.
[12] John 5. 20

hidden life, at once unique and infinite, there is a movement of love, also unique and infinite, of the two Persons, as it were face to face, who give themselves mutually and are united in so doing. And it is this reciprocal movement which is the Holy Spirit.

This is the light that is life, and the life that is light. It is this the Word came to reproduce amongst us, in our flesh and on our earth, in order that men might see it and live by it. This is what all those saw who were called by God to assist at our Lord's birth—the shepherds at the manger, the Wise Men at the humble dwelling at Bethlehem, Simeon and Anna in the Temple. It is this that filled them with complete joy.

Their faith did not falter at the sight of the poverty, the humbleness and the destitution, nor at the tiny being just born into this world without communion with created things. But this is only one side of the picture, the external aspect. The reality is a being in conscious and percipient contact with the whole of creation, with that world which belonged to him and of which he was the creator, the master. And it was this world that turned from him, that *knew him not*.[13] They saw a being turned entirely to *Him who is*, and away from all that *is not* and who, by that attitude, manifested truth and life. It was of this the shepherds sang as they returned to their sheep on the hillside; this

[13] Cf John I. 11.

CANDLEMAS

that caused the Wise Men to kneel at the foot of the divine Child's cradle; that drew from the soul of Simeon in the fullness of his joy his *Nunc dimittis* . . . [14], that plunged him into a profound peace. It was this that kept the two to whom that life was entrusted, Joseph and Mary, in a state of silent and constant adoration, of which the Gospel tells us nothing because it was beyond words.

But in order to realize this we, too, must turn to him, even as he is turned to the Father. Since the sin of our first parents mankind has been turned away from God, and we must turn back to him. God is there within us, but we have turned away and gone out of ourselves in order to find pleasure in created things. When we do enter into ourselves, we are content to stay in the superficial regions of our soul, in the lower or purely sensitive part; or, if we venture deeper into the more spiritual part, it is to the purely human layer, so to speak, which is governed by reason and our own will. This is what the Scriptures call *the darkness and the shadow of death*,[15] where there is agitation and trouble. If we would find peace, we must go deeper.

[14] Luke 2. 29.   [15] Luke 1. 79.

SIMEON

IN all the mysteries of the holy Childhood, you may have noticed an essential group of three persons who occupy the centre of the picture and are, as it were, its soul. These three we justly called the earthly trinity, a reflection of the most august Trinity in heaven —Jesus, Mary and Joseph. It is obvious that they must always invite and hold the major part of our attention; we shall never study them sufficiently; we shall never disclose completely the treasure of light hidden in these three simple figures. It is with them as with an horizon. To a child's inexperienced eye, an horizon appears quite close but, as one grows older, it seems to recede farther away, revealing fresh immensities to scan or new beauties to admire.

Nevertheless, by a loving design of which it is easy to guess the motives, the Holy Spirit has willed that quite near to them and in their light, there are other souls, and from these we can learn wonderful lessons. Such a one, in the mystery of the Purification of the Blessed Virgin, is the saintly old man Simeon, whom St Luke describes in a few words so admirably and succinctly.

There is a wonderful unity about his life,

and that is why it is so very striking and impressive. It is summed up in the word: he *waited: he was waiting for the consolation of Israel.*[1] This word, so sonorous in sound, is so full of meaning. He waited—that is to say, he was looking forward to something. He held all the energy of his being taut, concentrated and ordered, and he directed that energy towards one single end, an end that was the noblest that could be.

He was waiting for the Redeemer, who was to re-form souls in the image and likeness of God, souls deformed by sin. The Redeemer was that image, that likeness, that mirror that revealed traits of infinite beauty; that *figure of his substance,*[2] the brightness of eternal glory. He waited—intently—for *the desired of the nations.*[3] And in his ardour he had made for himself a picture of that form, that beauty and that splendour, of that light that had caused all other images to recede and alone held him in its grip. And so he waited...

This movement so strong, the end of which was so noble, had a cause indeed worthy of that end. *The Holy Ghost was in him.*[4] The Holy Spirit—that is to say, the very movement which in the Blessed Trinity held the Father and the Son eternally embraced in the same love, in the same gift of self which is their being and their life. This movement was

---

[1] Luke 2. 25.
[2] Heb. 1. 3.   [3] Cf. Agg. 2. 8.   [4] Luke 2. 25.

within him, and his waiting was this movement. But it was a movement subsequent to the Fall, after, that is, the separation caused by that Fall, when the sense of the loss engendered by it made him realize the sweetness of the severed relations, and the need to re-establish them.

To prepare him for this the Holy Spirit had done three things to him which are the indispensable conditions for reunion. First of all, he had inspired him with a perfect trust. *He had received an answer from the Holy Ghost that he should not see death before he had seen the Christ.*[5] For him that meant life, and it was for this he waited, for the fulfilment of that promise, of that understanding. It was this that kept him on the alert, and yet calm and assured, sure of God. And the Holy Spirit has added two dispositions which are no less necessary—justice and fear.

Ordinarily the word justice is derived from just, but in the Scriptures it has a much wider significance. It means, rather, perfect, and represents the whole, complete, ordered, harmonious, of all the virtues. It was the state of Adam before the Fall, and it is the state to which Christ, the New Adam, invites us when he says so unbelievably to his disciples: *Be you perfect, as also your heavenly Father is perfect.*[6] We do not think of this enough, and

[5] Luke 2. 26.
[6] Matt. 5. 48.

it is certain that we are far from putting it into practice.

A just man is someone, therefore, who is 'adjusted' to God. All his movements, and consequently all his powers which command or execute them, are in exact correspondence with what God wills. The state of a just man is such that he can say: *I do always the things that please* (God).[7] He reproduces that perfect justice of the perfect Just Man. Simeon was such a one. His being was perfectly adjusted, in tune like an instrument which, in the hands of a skilled artist, gives out always the required note. Simeon was just that, and yet he experienced a certain feeling of fear. It was not merely a passing feeling, but a state or disposition of the soul.

He was afraid—not of God. He was not afraid of the One he was expecting. On the contrary, he awaited him, he longed for him. He wanted nothing more than to be united with him. He had no fear that the Holy Spirit would not keep his promise; he was afraid of himself. He was afraid of his own weakness, of that wretchedness which has resulted from the Fall and which, inherent in his nature as in all of us, could not be relied upon. He knew that it was capable of not corresponding with the movements of the Holy Spirit, of not giving the exact note desired by the Master within him. He was afraid of the fragile vase in which,

[7] John 8. 29.

as St Paul says, we carry the precious treasure which is the very life of Christ.[8] He knew that, in spite of the presence of the Holy Spirit within him, the least false movement on his part could shatter that all too fragile vessel.

Thus, with perfect trust in God but mistrusting himself, filled with the Holy Spirit and entirely submissive to him in all his movements and powers, accustomed to be conscious of the slightest murmurs of the beloved voice, he awaited the realization of the divine promise, and that waiting was his whole life.

The issue of such a waiting is easy to foresee. On the day and at the hour when the interior voice said to him: 'He is there, he is in the Temple', all the co-ordinated energies of his being, the very muscles of his body and the powers of his soul, were released simply, without any effort, and combined to recognize and welcome the One he had so long desired. And from that more than contented soul, there arose the hymn of rest after toil, of possession after hope, the hymn of peace: *Now thou dost dismiss thy servant . . . in peace*; not, as is sometimes translated *Dismiss*, but *You may dismiss*.

For he makes no request; he is content, and more than content. His dearest wishes have been granted, and he is at peace. Not only is he at peace within himself (for peace fills his whole soul), but he is, as it were, plunged into

[8] Cf. 2 Cor. 4. 7. *But we have this treasure in earthen vessels.*

it like a vessel in deep waters. For peace is like a river,[9] indeed like a torrent. [10] It is the good measure, pressed down and running over, of which our Lord speaks.[11] Peace enfolds him and inundates his whole soul.

What a fitting end! We look for such a happiness also; we have the right to do so, and that peace can be ours, it should be ours. But we forget the waiting which must precede it, the long effort which is its preparation. The hour of peace, of rest, only sounds after the travail; it only sounds for those who have laboured,[12] who know how to prepare and make beautiful the inner sanctuary where the divine Visitor must come; who have long heard the voice of the Holy Spirit and, in order to hear him, have turned from all other voices; who know how to welcome the expected Redeemer when he comes.

---

[9] Cf. Isa. 48. 18. *Thy peace had been as a river, and thy justice as the waves of the sea.*
[10] Cf. Ps. 35. 9. *Thou shalt make them drink of the torrent of thy pleasure.* [11] Cf. Luke 6. 38.
[12] Cf. Matt. 11. 28. *Come to me, all you that labour.*

ASCENSION

THE life of our Lord presents a unity in which all the parts are connected and explain one another. It is that unity the Psalmist describes when he compares it to the course of the sun in the heavens. *His going out is from the end of heaven, and his circuit even to the end thereof*,[1] he says, and it is to the 'end of heaven' that he returns after having illumined and warmed our earth. Both the dawn and the sunset are 'at the ends of the earth', and both are the loveliest one can imagine. But between the two there is a hard way, which must be traversed—his Passion and death.

This is what our Lord himself explains on the evening of the day of his resurrection on the way to Emmaus, to the discouraged disciples who failed to recognize him. *We had hoped*, they said, *that it was he that should have redeemed Israel*,[2] but the high-priests condemned him to death, and already it is the third day. And Jesus, still without making himself known, replied: O slow of heart, to understand and believe. That Cross, that death—they were necessary; it was the only way to arrive at his glory... This was God's plan, which he had announced by his prophets.

[1] Ps. 18. 7. [2] Luke 24. 21.

And, beginning with Moses, continues the evangelist, he unfolded and explained to them the long series of prophecies connecting his sorrowful Passion with his entry into his glory.[3]

Our Lord was not content merely to mention this connection, hard and necessary as it was; he explained it and gave the real reason for it. His explanation is the summary of the whole of the Gospel, which would be meaningless without it. Open the Gospel where you will, and you will find it on every page. The clearest and fullest reference to it is in our Lord's discourse after the Last Supper, when Judas, at last unmasked and having left the Upper Room in order to deliver him to the Jews, Jesus had to tell the apostles that the hour had come when he must suffer. *I will not now speak many things with you,* he told them, *for the prince of this world cometh* . . .[4] It is not that he has any rights over me, he has absolutely none whatever. It is solely *that the world may know that I love the Father.*[5]

Union with his Father; the manifestation of that union, of that movement of love, of the breathing of the Holy Spirit—this was the reason for and the true nature of his Passion. It is an ascension which restores him to the Father, and whereby he re-enters into his glory.

He is sad because the world does not understand this. *That the world may know;* that the

[3] Cf. Luke 24. 26.   [4] John 14. 30.   [5] John 14. 31.

'breathing' of the Holy Spirit may be made manifest; that it may be known and communicated to those who will understand and see. And so, when he spoke in advance of his Passion, when he announced it, he called it always a 'lifting-up', an *ascension*. He explained this to Nicodemus at the beginning of his public life when he said: *As Moses lifted up the serpent in the desert, so must the Son of man be lifted up.*[6] And all those who in that 'lifting up' are able to see the eternal union of the Father and the Son shall share in that union and shall enter into that life. He repeated the same idea in almost the same words to the Jews when he came on his last visit to Jerusalem for the Paschal feast: *And I, if I be lifted up from the earth, will draw all men to me.*[7] And on that same day he repeated it even more clearly: *Amen, amen, I say to you: unless the grain of wheat falling into the ground die, itself remaineth alone. But if it die, it bringeth forth much fruit.*[8]

His Passion and death are, nevertheless, but passing realities, on the surface, as it were, of things—we might almost say mere appearances. The deep reality is the life which is renewed, the new tree which comes to life. It is his ascension, destined to bear fruit, into that rarer atmosphere which is his real dwelling-place, his Father's bosom.[9] But what is the reason for this?

[6] John 3. 14.   [7] Cf. John 12. 32.   [8] John 12. 24-25.
[9] Cf. John 1. 18. *The only-begotten who is in the bosom of the Father.*

It is because, in falling into the ground, the tiny grain comes into contact with the nourishing element from which it was formed. The earth into which it falls is its proper sphere. In our Lord's case, his 'sphere' is the bosom of the Father; his Passion and death prelude his return to that bosom. What fell and died was only the outer protective covering, needed for the time of formation and growth. Once that growth had been assured, the outer covering must disappear; it must burst asunder to make way for life. The covering or shell is but a tombstone; the risen spirit removes it.

It is this spirit, this deep movement, which is communicated again to the body on that Easter morning. But this time, since Christ had no longer to resemble us in suffering and death, he assimilated it to himself completely by making it a spiritualized body; he communicated his movement of life to it. And one day, when he deemed that the time had come, in the presence of the apostles and disciples gathered together, so as to fulfil the divine plan and make known his Father's power, that power raised him up gently and bore him to the bosom of his Father.[10]

This is what we celebrate today. It is the end, the glorious crowning, the striking manifestation of the movement of the spirit of love which animated the whole of the life and activity of Jesus, and which he came to

[10] Cf. Luke 24. 51.

reveal. But in order to be aware of that spirit we must possess it. The apostles had not as yet received it; and that is why, in spite of our Lord's recommendation to them,[11] they loitered, looking up at that body and at the cloud that slowly hid it from their sight. And the angel had to say to them: *Why stand you looking up to heaven?*[12] Under that visible form Christ had achieved his mission;[13] he had given us all that he had to give.

What we have to do now is to give ourselves up entirely to this love which had animated his life. We must plunge ourselves, immerse ourselves, in this spirit as in waters that will make us new men. Moved by this sacred spirit, we also must, after our Lord's example, make that slow ascension, following the way he followed. For, as St Paul tells us, we are called to re-enter with him into the bosom of the Father, there to reign eternally with him. But we can only reign with him, if we have suffered with him.[14]

---

[11] Cf. John 14. 26. *But the Paraclete, the Holy Ghost, whom the Father will send in my name, he will teach you all things...*

[12] Acts 1. 11.

[13] Cf. John 17. 4. *I have finished the work which thou gavest me to do.*

[14] Cf. 2 Tim. 2. 12. *If we suffer (with him) we shall also reign with him.*

PENTECOST

GOD is love. It is his name, the name he gave himself among us, the last and consequently the definitive expression of his being, the true light in which he wishes us to see him.

It is very specially the name that belongs to his life, and to that intimate movement which comes from the depths of his being; which is, as it were, the breathing, the respiration that takes place in the three Persons, of whom he is the act and life. In himself, as outside of himself, he sees only this: he wants only this, he does only this—he loves and gives himself. In himself, this gift is infinite and therefore eternal—eternally perfect and complete. Outside of himself, it acts by successive communications, for it is addressing itself to 'nothingness' which can only receive him in the measure of the being that he imparts to it.

Today, we celebrate the last of these external communications. As in all cases of 'endings' this last communication lights up and explains all the other communications. But it cannot be understood unless it is seen in the light of the whole that it crowns and consummates.

These external communications of the spirit of God, these effusions of divine love outside of himself, commenced with creation[1] and fills its history. In the beginning, says the Book of Genesis, the earth was void—it was an abyss, a chaotic and formless mass, without light or life. *And the spirit of God moved over the waters.*[2] The abyss had some kind of appearance, and it was to that appearance that the spirit of God addressed itself. It acted on it, and accomplished in the act proper to it which is the gift of itself. It *moved over the waters*; it communicated to them that warmth and fire, which is its form, and under that action wrested them from the abyss and raised them up and, turning them, drew them towards itself. Little by little, it made them less dense, it made them mobile, light, aery, transparent and, as it were, spiritualized.

Then gradually in turn it wrested from the abyss the more consistent mass of the firm earth, and then the living germs it contained, drawing them also to itself. By them it spread in the air all that it had of light and warmth, and in the soil the living sap. With these it formed the plants, the living organisms with their colours and scents, and that strange reality, life already reproducing itself.

By the animals on the earth and the birds in the air, the fishes in the sea; by their organs of sensibility and their movements in space which allow them to enter into contact with all this lower creation, the spirit of God

[1] Cf. Gen. 1, *passim*.   [2] Gen. 1. 2.

pursues its work of communication, giving itself to all creatures. It makes of them a *whole*, an immense chain of connecting links, whereby all give themselves to one another and thus realize the plan of love and unity of him who gives himself in them, and teaches them to give themselves.

They give themselves, but they know it not. To give oneself without knowing or willing it is not really to give oneself; it is only a kind of shadow, a trial sketch of love. The spirit of God wants more than that; it wants true reflections, beings who give themselves as it gives itself. God said: *Let us make man to our image and likeness.*[3] Then, continues the Book of Genesis, *God formed man of the slime of the earth,*[4] and so brought him within that created whole. And he breathed into him that breath which is life, that same breath which he breathed over the waters. And man, made in his image and likeness, was able to give himself as God gives himself, and is thus capable of true love.

And man refused. He did not know how to raise himself up out of the soil, to lift himself above himself. He kept the breath of God to himself, that breath which, coming from him must return to him. By making man free, God foresaw and allowed for this opposition, and so prepared a supreme communication of his

[3] Gen. 1. 26.
[4] Gen. 2. 7.

love, which was to be its most wonderful manifestation.

The creation of man in a state of grace makes us, according to the word of St Peter, *partakers of the divine nature*.[5] This is a nameless privilege that we shall never really understand in this life. But there is still something more, and divine Love, while remaining free, wills to love to the end. He wills that perfect *gift of self* which is a union, not only of nature but a personal union, whereby human nature and a divine Person are made one.

This also is the work of the spirit of God. The angel of the Annunciation said to our Lady: *The Holy Ghost shall come upon thee ... and the Holy which shall be born of thee shall be called the Son of God*,[6] the Son begotten before the dawn of the world by the full communication of the spirit of the Father. For three and thirty years that spirit was communicating its fullness to that nature united to the Word, and he made thus a perfect man, the résumé of all creation. Through his body he unites himself to the whole of material creation, he gives himself to all and in so doing is joined to all.[7] Before giving himself he again immerses himself therein, taking the form of bread and wine. Thus formed and united to all, thereby manifesting freely and lovingly what he is and what he does and how he gives himself, he gives

---

[5] 2 Pet. 1. 4.   [6] Luke 1. 35.
[7] 1 Cor. 6. 17. *But he who is joined to the Lord is one spirit.*

back all with himself into the hands of the Father, making all re-enter by love into that bosom of the Father, which is the source of all. *Into thy hands I commend my spirit.*[8]

This is the spirit that animates and unites and is the beauty of that holy City, the New Jerusalem, of which St John traces so magnificent a picture,[9] and whose feast we keep today. He is himself that city and the glory of it. He is the adornment and beauty of the bride, the spirit of the Lamb immolated. And as Jesus had received that spirit with his body and his human nature, in the womb of the Virgin who gave herself as he gives himself, so he manifested it throughout the whole of his life on earth. His Passion was its supreme demonstration, and had no other meaning. He gave this spirit to the world so that he might thus take possession of those souls that are prepared to reproduce his image; and he eternally shines in them as a sun they so perfectly reflect.

Meanwhile, he prepares them by purifying them. And he purifies them by drawing them to himself by turning them away from all that is not himself. He makes them hear always the sweet voice of Love as St John heard it saying: Come, leave yourselves; come out of yourselves—*come* . . .[10] And the spirit repeats it unceasingly, until he accomplishes that perfect

[8] Luke 23. 46.
[9] Cf. Apoc. 21 and 22, *passim*.
[10] Apoc. 22. 17. *And the Spirit and the bride say: Come.*

union of which the beloved disciple speaks. They say it together, in the eternal present as with one voice, and they live the same word, eternally realized and renewed, which is the end and purpose of all the divine communications: *Come!*...

ST JOHN THE BAPTIST

ST JOHN the Baptist occupies in the Gospel and in Christian devotion a place apart. This is only as it should be, for twice God himself willed to make known his greatness. The angel Gabriel, in announcing his birth said formally in the name of heaven: *He shall be great.*[1] Three and thirty years later, when he was in prison, having fulfilled his mission, the Master said of him to the crowd: *There hath not risen among them that are born of women a greater than John the Baptist.*[2] The whole of his life was lived between these two attestations of his greatness.

That greatness was not just a mere human greatness, the kind of natural superiority to which the world attaches far too much importance. It was not the greatness of a day, more or less artificial and often purely artificial, which even, when it is real, is always very inferior. Of the greatness of St John the Baptist the angel said explicitly: *He shall be great before the Lord.*[3] His greatness was to be such that it would be able to stand the gaze of the God of truth, and it need not fear the light of his countenance. Our Lord made this very clear to the Jews when he said to them:

[1] Luke I. 15.   [2] Matt. II. 11.   [3] Luke I. 15.

What went you out into the desert to see? A reed shaken with the wind?[4]—that is to say, a man at the mercy of the capricious movements of human opinion, more vacillating than the reeds by the side of the river running close by. Was it to see *a man clothed in soft garments*,[5] eager for all that flatters the senses? No! You came to see a prophet, a man of God, who sees everything and everyone in the divine light which appraises them according to the glory they give to God. Our Lord could speak thus, for the greatness of the Baptist was his work; he was responsible for it entirely, from the first moment of his life to the last.

In order to explain the mysterious movement that she experienced in her womb when our Lady, shortly after the Annunciation, came to visit her, Elizabeth the mother of John, used a very expressive word; she said: *The infant in my womb leaped for joy.*[6] For at that moment, a ray from the womb of Mary, from him who is the Light of whom John was later to be the heroic witness, illumined the soul of the Precursor. In the little being, scarcely conceived, whom the Virgin carried in her bosom, it showed him the Lord, the Master, whom the angel of the Annunciation called *The Son of the most High*;[7] whose glory fills the earth and the heavens, and whose love draws and gives life to souls. And before that

[4] Matt. 11. 7.
[5] Matt. 11. 8.   [6] Luke 1. 44.   [7] Luke 1. 32.

light, before that love, that glory and that life, John's soul leaped. Its movement communicated itself to that tiny body still in formation, and it also leaped. It did this in order to rejoin a certain object, to make contact with him, to place himself in the presence of this Master, and so realize the inhabitation that our Lord described and asked for when he said: *Abide in me.*[8] Thus these two souls were united, they penetrated one another; the soul of John became in truth the dwelling-place of Jesus, and there were initiated relations altogether spiritual which were to persist to the end. And John remained in that sacred thrill of possession, in that presence and in that union, and never ceased responding to it. It lifted him up, and *he leaped with joy*, in order to maintain that contact and make it all the stronger.

His whole life was this movement of which the prophet Isaias spoke when, in a beautiful text which we repeat often during Advent, he speaks of that summit where God dwells, and towards which the hills are drawn.[9] He compares this movement to the flowing of a river following its course: *All nations shall flow unto it.*[10] The whole life of John was just that—a flowing, a movement full, total and simple, where all the little drops of life tend to

---

[8] John 15 4.
[9] Cf. Isa. 2. 2. *And in the last days the mountain of the house of the Lord shall be prepared on the top of mountains, and it shall be exalted above the hills.*
[10] Isa. 2. 2. *And all nations shall flow unto it.*

the loved object which draws them. His life hymned that greatness, and reflected its traits. And this object was within him, in the depths of his soul, and it was there that object held him.

These external manifestations, these stages in the movement of life, are interesting; some of them even abound for us in profitable lessons. For instance, those long years of contemplation in the desert, where for him was realized to the full the words of Jeremias: *He shall sit solitary, and hold his peace.*[11] The solitary keeps under control all futile agitation; he silences all useless noises and rises superior to himself. He makes himself greater than himself, great with that true greatness which will be given him.

Nevertheless these manifestations are only on the surface; they are merely what we see of his life, and it is necessary to pass beyond them. It is the One he is looking at who is the soul, the motive force and the heart of his life: that interior and deep movement which sustains him. It is what he himself explained in words more beautiful even than those of the prophets, words impregnated with an unheard-of tenderness, the tenderness of the New Covenant. They are his last. His disciples complained that our Lord was baptizing on his own, and that all were flocking to him. And John replied: *He is the Bridegroom, I am but*

[11] Lam. 3. 28.

his friend.[12] The role of a friend consists in keeping close to the Bridegroom, and his sole joy is to hear him.[13] And so he added: *He that believeth in the Son hath life everlasting.*[14]

Here we have arrived at the extreme depth of John's soul, and at the summit of his greatness. The divine 'leaping' began in his mother's womb; it followed him to the desert, in his public preaching. That divine thrill, which had been his life, ended there, at the Bridegroom's side, hearing his voice. There he found his rest and happiness, convinced that, under the rule of faith and in this earth's shadows, it is truly eternal life, begun already here below. He that believeth in the Son *hath* life everlasting.

---

[12] Cf. John 3. 29.
[13] Cf. John 3. 29. *This my joy therefore is fulfilled.*
[14] John 3. 36.

ALL SAINTS

THE feast of All Saints sums up all other feasts, and is their crown. The Office of the feast is very beautiful, and is manifestly composed in this sense and with this end in view. In that Office, the Church bids us praise first *Him who is*, by whom all things are, from whom we receive all moment by moment and who, in giving us his Son who is his life, has become our Father. Then we praise the divine Son himself, but under the human form with which he clothed himself so that we might find him in that sweet and glorious relation as children of God. Then we sing to Mary who shares with the heavenly Father the privilege of having begotten the Son, and who gives birth to him unceasingly in us, if we wish it, and who is thus ever our Mother. Then, in ordered groups at once distinct yet united, like God himself, we praise the countless multitude of those—prophets and apostles, martyrs, confessors and virgins—who bear on their foreheads the paternal sign, the blood of the Lamb slain.[1]

The Church's intention on this day is thus clear. She wishes us to pass it wholly with heaven's entire company. That is why she

[1] Cf. Apoc. 14. 1.

makes us read the splendid passage where the beloved disciple, admitted, in the evening of his long life, to the contemplation of the divine mystery, describes to us that company, that heavenly family, which wants so intensely to become our family. His description, for which he can only use earthly words, is clearly very far from the reality. It gives only a very poor representation of it. Imperfect as it is, nevertheless it represents all that we ought to know of that life which will one day be our life.

His picture is that of an immense city, where all is plenitude and perfection. The number twelve, the perfect number, is found there again and again. A wall of twelve times twelve thousand cubits surrounds the city and it rested on twelve foundations and had twelve gates.[1] And, guarding these gates, were twelve angels, and on the gates were inscribed the names of the twelve tribes of Israel. Twelve thousand men of each tribe occupy that New Jerusalem, where God re-assembles the elect. All mourning, all sorrow, all that can in any-way hurt our human sensitivity, is banished from it. *And God shall wipe away all tears from their eyes, and death shall be no more, nor mourning, nor sorrow*[2]—all will have been wiped away by the hand of God. All the riches of the earth, all the splendours of creation, all that is the delight of the eyes, all that charms

[1] Cf. Apoc. 21. 12ff.   [2] Apoc. 21. 4.

and captivates the senses, all that can enchant and satisfy us is there united. All there is pure, limpid crystal, radiant light... and this, not just by way of adornment, a mere superficial covering. The walls of the city, the city itself, its heart and setting, are made of it.[4]

In its centre is a throne, and on this throne someone is seated.[5] St John does not tell us his name, he simply says what he does. For his name is his being, and his being is his act. He is essential *Gift of self*. He is love, he is light, and he radiates that light; from him flows a river,[6] and this river bears with it life which spreads to all and everything. And in the midst is a tree, whose fruits preserve that life in its integrity and plenitude.[7] And there shall be no sun nor moon, nor stars nor temple, for he is all these things, and takes their place.[8]

And on the same throne, at once distinct yet one with him, is the Lamb. The river of light and love which flows from the bosom of the Father is seen first of all in him as in a immense mirror, which receives him fully and communicates him to others. He is his perfect image, the radiating splendour which reflects him, thus making him visible and available to men. All life is in him, and he gives out that

---

[4] Apoc. 21. 21.
[5] Cf. Apoc. 4. 2. *And behold, there was a throne set in heaven, and upon the throne one sitting.*
[6] Apoc. 22. 1. *And he shewed me a river of water of life.*
[7] Apoc. 22. 2. *And in the midst...was the tree of life.*
[8] Apoc. 22. 5. See Also Apoc. 21. 23. *The Lamp is the lamp thereof.*

life; all light is in him and he spreads it. For ever and to all men he repeats: *I am the light of the world. He that followeth me walketh not in darkness, but shall have the light of life.*[9]

The elect are there, facing the throne, facing him who occupies it and who is being, light and life; facing the Lamb who reproduces that being, light and life. The elect are clothed in the nuptial robe, which is the blood of the Lamb slain. He has washed that robe and clothes them and adorns them with it.[10] He has given it that purity which is detachment; no created stain spoils that purity or can intercept the light that comes from God. To these chosen souls Jesus the Lamb gives above all that white and virginal brightness, that light of love which is a reflection of God's own brightness and beauty; they become themselves mirrors of God. From them also comes a ray, a ray which they have received and which has become their being and life. And this ray returns—always through the divine Mediator, the Lamb slain—to its first Principle, to him who is seated on the throne. This ray is the hymn of their whole being; they sing it unceasingly to him who is seated on the throne and to the Lamb: *Benediction and glory and wisdom and thanksgiving, honour and power and strength, to our God, for ever and ever, amen.*[11]

---

[9] John 8. 12.
[10] Cf. Apoc. 7. 14. *These are they who have washed their robes and have made them white in the blood of the Lamb.*
[11] Apoc. 7. 12.

Then is realized the divine prayer of the Cenacle: *Father, I will that where I am, they also whom thou hast given me may be with me;*[12] that they may see the light of love in which I was in thee before the world was, in order that they may be consummated in our unity, *I in them and thou in me . . . that they may see my glory,*[13] and that it may become their glory. Even now, under the veil of faith, in the secret depths of souls, in that mysterious retreat where God gives himself, the divine mystery which will restore to us eternal happiness is already on earth unrolled. The Father is there; he sees us, he calls us. His Holy Spirit is there to guide us to the sources of the waters of true life. All heaven is there, and awaits us.

But we—where are we? Are we 'before the throne of God'? Is there not another throne; have we broken down all our idols? Has the blood of the Lamb, the total sacrifice without reserve, purified us completely? Have our thoughts become so detached that they are concentrated solely on the one object necessary?[14] Are all the chords of our harps, all the powers of our being, in tune? Do they vibrate with one single note, the note of love? Do we offer to God all our honours, all that we have of being, of character and of merit?

One day we shall see a name written in heaven. This name will be the universal one of

---

[12] John 17. 24.
[13] John 17. 23-24.   [14] Cf. Luke 10. 42.

Father, to which by our acts we shall give the form, personal and unique, which will be our own name. This name will shine for all eternity on our foreheads.[15] Our Lord was thinking of this name when he said: *I will call my sheep by their name.*[16] It is the name pronounced by that divine voice, which will make us thrill with eternal happiness. Of this name, there will appear in heaven only what we have written in him and by him. All the rest, as Holy Scripture says, is written on earth.[17] A gust of wind will pass, and carry all away...

Ah, if we could but write only such words as will live! But for this, we must write them 'before the throne of our heavenly Father', for his glory—with and in the blood of the Lamb.

---

[15] Cf. Apoc. 14. 1. *Having his name and the name of the Father written on their foreheads.*

[16] John 10. 2-3. Cf. also John 10. 14. *I am the good shepherd, and I know mine and mine know me.*

[17] Cf. Eccles. 3. 20. *Of earth they were made, and into earth they return together.*

www.ingramcontent.com/pod-product-compliance
Lightning Source LLC
Chambersburg PA
CBHW031943070426
42450CB00006BA/807